DIAGNOSE YOUR FINANCIAL HEALTH

By

Dr. Wendy Labat
The Financial Healer

*To Jira "The Gratitude Specialist,"
We've come a long way since the Media Mastery Boot Camp despite COVID-19. I'm so proud of you & how you pivoted to empower others to soar. Happy to be a part of your team. I appreciate your support!!
Thanks!!
Dr. Wendy*

Diagnose Your Financial Health
by Dr. Wendy Labat
Copyright 2020

All rights reserved. No part of this book may be reproduced, stored in a retrieval system, or transmitted in any form or by any means – electronic, mechanical, photocopying, recording or otherwise—without written permission from Dr. Edwina Labat, except for the inclusion of quotations.

We have made all attempts to verify information provided in this book and assume no responsibility for errors, omissions, or contrary interpretation of the subject matter. Any perceived slights of specific persons or organizations are purely unintentional.

There are no guarantees of results. Readers are cautioned to use their own judgment about their circumstances and act accordingly.

This book is not intended for use as a source for accounting, financial, business, or legal advice. Readers are advised to seek the services of competent professionals in those fields.

Unless otherwise indicated, all scriptures are taken from the King James Version (KJV).

Requests for permission and other inquiries should be addressed to:

The Financial Cures LLC
PO Box 943
Fayetteville, GA 30214
Email: info@thefinancialcures.com

Printed in the United States of America
ISBN: 9798681376187

What Others Are Saying...

While anyone possessing the requisite knowledge can write a book on home budgeting and financing, it takes a special person to do so with genuine care and concern for those who will read it. Such is the case with Dr. Edwina (Wendy) Labat in this easy-to-read, intelligently practical manuscript entitled, Diagnose Your Financial Health. *I know for a fact that she has a heart for people because I personally have asked her on numerous occasions to assist others in dealing with financial structuring and upheaval in their lives, and she has come through admirably by listening to their situations and offering sound, usable advice that helps them out of their confused or stressed predicaments.*

Truly, I believe she has what we identify in the faith world as a calling upon her life—that is, a divine sanction, an anointing, to assist others with their financial matters, which, when left unattended, can cause so much disharmony and strife in families and communities. Dr. Labat's book is worth reading, not only because it provides extremely helpful information but also because it is, in so many ways, the moving testimony of a woman of faith.

Aaron L. Parker, PhD
Pastor, Zion Hill Baptist Church
Associate Professor, Morehouse College

Dr. Wendy Labat takes readers on a dark, twisted, and truthful journey into the perilous world of their financial condition. This message is a homerun! Dr. Wendy has written a must-read primer for anyone ready to take control over their finances, achieve financial freedom, and live the life they desire. Read this book — and learn from one of the best.

**Che Brown, Host of Happy Entrepreneur Show,
#1 Business Development Late Night Show,
and Founder of Champion Nation**

Dr. Wendy Labat, aka The Financial Healer, not only talks the talk, she has walked the walk on the path of financial health. With over 20 years of expertise and experience, she has helped individuals from all walks of life overcome the obstacles to optimizing their financial health. Diagnose Your Financial Health *will help shift your current mental mindset to see what is possible in the future of your finances.*

Linda Clemons, CEO of Sisterpreneur® Inc.

TABLE OF CONTENTS

- DEDICATION VII
- ACKNOWLEDGMENTS IX
- FOREWORD XI
- PREFACE XIII
- INTRODUCTION 17
- 1. THE SIX OBSTACLES TO OPTIMIZE YOUR FINANCIAL HEALTH 23
- 2. BASIC TERMS, DEFINITIONS, AND PRINCIPLES 37
- 3. VITAL SIGNS AND SYMPTOMS 51
  - INCOME 52
  - EXPENSES 54
  - SPENDING 56
  - SPENDING CHALLENGE 57
- 4. CREATIVE WAYS TO INCREASE YOUR INCOME 61
  - CASH-BACK, REWARDS, & LOYALTY PROGRAMS 62
  - COUPONS, FREE TRIALS, DISCOUNTS, AND BOGO 63
  - SELL PRODUCTS ONLINE 64
- 5. REDUCE EXPENSES WITHOUT SPENDING MORE MONEY 69
  - AVOID LATE FEES AND PENALTIES 70
  - OVERDRAFT FEES 70
  - EVALUATE AND RENEGOTIATE 71
  - CANCEL UNUSED MEMBERSHIPS & SUBSCRIPTIONS 72
  - CONSOLIDATE/ REFINANCE LOANS 74
  - REWARDS, CASH BACK, COUPONS, DISCOUNTS, AND OFFERS 75
- 6. CHECK YOUR SIGHT 79
- 7. WHAT IS YOUR DIAGNOSIS? 85
- CONCLUSION 89
- ABOUT THE AUTHOR 95
- FREE GIFT 97

DEDICATION

This book is dedicated to my family. My great-grandmother, Mrs. Jesse Martin, who encouraged me at a young age to get a college education or, as she put it, "bump my head on the college walls."

My grandparents, Governor and Hortense Blackwell, who instilled the importance of entrepreneurship, etiquette, and manners to achieve success in life and business.

My parents, Edward and Ruby White, who ingrained the importance of self-confidence, respect for myself and others.

My husband, Carl, who is my rock. My children, Erika, Craig, and Cedric, who have been my motivation to be an excellent example for them to follow. I am so proud of the responsible, confident, and respectful, individuals they have become.

My sister, Tanya, is my support and sounding board. My grandchildren, Mekhi and Kailyn, who I love dearly and look forward to seeing them grow up to be fine adults. My fur baby, Angel, who brings me joy every day.

ACKNOWLEDGMENTS

The Blessed Trinity, thank you for putting me on this path for my life. You always make a way when there does not seem to be a way. When you give me a vision, you also give me the provision to see it through. Continue to direct and light my path throughout this journey called life.

Pamela Warner, thanks for your loyalty, dedication, and friendship throughout the years. You were there with me in the beginning and stuck with me through thick and thin. Your encouragement and faith in me kept me going, especially when things got tough. Look at us now. We made it.

Terry Clark Sr., my trusted advisor and friend. You are the reason I discovered the "financial cure" for breast cancer. Your counsel and direction prompted me to acquire the proper protection that prevented my financial ruin after I was diagnosed and treated for breast cancer. Not only did I survive, but I also thrived. Thanks for your leadership.

Patricia Clark, "The Closer." You planted the seed for me to write a book. Although I shunned the idea, God watered that seed and this book is the harvest I have reaped. Thanks for your confidence in me.

LaChelle Adkins, America's Super Mom. Thank you for reaching out to me and inviting me to be a part of your workshops. Look what you started! I am on a roll! :) Thanks for your support.

Sylvia Morris, you have been my right hand, a loyal, honest, and trustworthy friend who I can always count on. God truly blessed me when He sent you into my life. Thanks for having my back!

FOREWORD

Let me start by saying if you are looking to learn from a master in her industry, Dr. Wendy Labat is your person when it comes to taking ownership of your financial destiny. As you learn about her story, you will learn she has faced every challenge imaginable and has overcome them. I have learned working directly with her for the past couple of years that she is a person of her word and always over-delivers with her clients.

This book will guide you through the challenging times we are currently living with grace and style. Her process of proper financial planning to make sure you have the proper insurance to protect your livelihood is a must-read for everyone ages 18–80. The toughest conversations revolve around the hard questions that we always forget to ask when it comes to dealing with devastation in your finances.

Imagine being able to read one book that will be your guide for the next 20–30 years. It is just one reason that you should not only read this book but share it with everyone you can think of in your family and network of friends and business associates. As you will learn, when you complete this book, it will serve as a great guide for navigating your financial future.

Many of the tips, concepts, and ideas that are covered in the book, I have actually watched Dr. Wendy share from our stages all across America. I would also highly recommend if you get a chance to work with her on any other programs or courses she offers, take advantage of that offer as soon as possible!

Great job, Dr. Wendy Labat. I am so proud of you!

Bill Walsh
CEO/Founder
Powerteam International

PREFACE

The first time I heard Dr. Wendy share her story in front of an audience, I knew immediately that this was a woman of integrity and faith, and her story would be shared over and over again. We were both speaking at the same event, and Dr. Wendy's stage presence was glamorous, warm, and inviting—the opposite of what you would think a financial presentation would be.

When Dr. Wendy talks about buying insurance products for herself as a way to talk with her clients, you instantly grasp the amount of trust she brings to every professional and personal relationship. She walks her walk and draws people in.

You know you are in the presence of a woman walking in faith when she shares her journey of having those same insurance products in place during her own personal medical crisis. It was not a coincidence. Dr. Wendy thought she was being practical when she responded to a very strong urge inside of her to have these products in place. You cannot help but recognize that God knew her story would have an impact. So after seeing her on stage, sharing her journey in such a brave and authentic way, I could not wait for her book to come out.

Dr. Wendy has designed one of the most comprehensive lessons on budgeting, building wealth, and protecting your finances on the market today. She has personally walked through the lessons, brought it to her clients, and is now providing her wisdom and knowledge in this book for all the world to have at their fingertips.

They say that most businesses fail due to a lack of finances. Most broken families claim it was due to financial troubles. Financial troubles attract even more struggles, especially when there is a medical crisis you cannot bounce back from. Yet a few basic changes to what you know about money can protect you from a financial crisis. Dr. Wendy starts with the very basics of handling money, all throughout building a financial legacy and creating generational wealth.

When my husband and I first married, we each brought our own financial history and experience into the mix—neither of us had a clue about budgeting, investing, or insurance. We learned through trial and error. As newlyweds, the words "financial legacy" were not in our vocabulary. We almost filed for bankruptcy due to extended medical bills when our twins were born.

It was not until we jumped into the world of entrepreneurship that we were even exposed to some of the lessons Dr. Wendy teaches. Being an entrepreneur requires hard and quick lessons in finances. The lessons we learned the "hard way" are all summed up in

The Financial Cures System™ starting with *Diagnose Your Financial Health*.

Dr. Wendy is a creative financial teacher. She is a trusted friend and colleague. Her guidance is designed to walk you step-by-step into creating stable financial health. Just as you take care of your personal health by staying active and watching what you eat, our financial health requires an active approach too.

I have enjoyed watching Wendy put her creative spin on diagnosing and optimizing financial health. It is a creative approach to baby step your way to financial success. I am still in the audience learning lessons from this wonderful woman.

Cheers!

Angel Tuccy
Best Selling Author
ABC's of Exposure

INTRODUCTION

Are you a faithful servant over your finances? Many people think getting more money will be the answer to all their problems. In reality, understanding how money works, knowing how to manage money, no matter the amount, and making money work for you is the real solution. If you do not manage and control what you have now, how will you manage and control more?

> *Well done, thou good and faithful servant: thou hast been faithful over a few things, I will make thee ruler over many things.*
> *– Matthew 25:21 –*

Most people keep a written record of their income and expenses but overlook their spending. Uncontrolled spending can prevent you from paying for the essential things you need, reduce/eliminate debt, build an emergency fund/cash reserves, and become financially free. Detailed tracking of your income, expenses, and most importantly, your spending helps you see a realistic picture of your financial situation.

The objective is to plan where your money goes instead of wondering where it went.

> *Write the vision and make it plain.*
> *– Habakkuk 2:2 –*

To achieve your financial goals, you must know your current financial situation. Once you have a realistic picture, no matter how good or bad, it takes three essential elements to move forward. You must decide, commit, and take action to achieve your financial goals. Your mindset and discipline require the transformation of your thinking and habits as they relate to your desired level of achievement. You cannot want a rich man's wealth and have a poor man's mentality.

> *But be ye transformed by the renewing of your mind.*
> *– Romans 12:2 –*

> *For as he thinketh in his heart, so is he.*
> *– Proverbs 23:7 –*

This book was written to empower people to overcome the obstacles to winning the money game and achieve optimum financial health. Many professional women and entrepreneurs are responsible for the financial well-being of their families and business. It can be a struggle if you do not have the mindset, knowledge, and tools to take control over your finances and make your money work for you.

People ask me what makes me an expert financial strategist. Let me begin with my entrepreneurial journey that started over 36 years ago. I started a business with no experience and very limited financial resources. This was a time when there was no internet or social media, and the only thing you could do with a cell phone was make an expensive phone call.

My clients were major corporations. To be considered for the big contracts, my company had to project the right image. That meant having a brick and mortar office, employees, inventory, and all the overhead that goes with it. If you projected anything less, your company was perceived as a mom and pop operation not capable of handling big contracts.

Times were tough because my cash flow did not match my overhead expenses. Payroll, rent, utilities, and other expenses had to be paid whether the company made money or not. The more sales and contracts the company acquired, the more inventory had to be purchased to fulfill the contracts.

My limited financial resources forced me to think outside the box to meet my expenses. I used creative ways to increase revenue, improve cash flow, and position my company for growth and development. This experience taught me how to take control over my finances, make my money work for me, get my clients to pay my company sooner rather than later, and continue to find creative ways to acquire the things needed to expand my business.

In 2014, when the Affordable Care Act mandated that everyone have healthcare coverage, I expanded my business to include insurance products and financial services. Not wanting to be a hypocrite, I believed if I was going to sell my clients these products and services, I needed to acquire them for myself and my family. So I purchased all the products I was selling. This was done as part of a marketing and business strategy, not from a personal financial planning perspective.

In 2017, I was diagnosed with breast cancer and underwent five surgeries. My chemotherapy infusions were every three weeks for a year, at a cost of $67,000 every three weeks. Additionally, the cost of the five surgeries, CAT scans, MRIs, ultrasounds, mammograms, and lab tests exceeded $300,000. Can you imagine having to pay those kinds of expenses in addition to your personal and business expenses while battling breast cancer?

The cost of treating this disease could have ruined me and my family financially. Thank God I practiced what I preached. My health insurance paid all of my medical bills. Plus, the supplemental coverage I purchased paid a significant tax-free payout that allowed me to focus on my recovery without worrying about money. I considered this The Financial Cure and hence, The Financial Cures System™ was developed.

Subsequently, I began my crusade to empower others with The Financial Cures System™ to take control over their finances, make their money work for them, acquire proper protection to prevent financial ruin, build a financial legacy, create generational wealth, enjoy financial freedom, and live the life they desire. Let us start the process to diagnose your financial health.

Chapter One
THE SIX OBSTACLES TO OPTIMIZE YOUR FINANCIAL HEALTH

The path to optimizing your financial health can be filled with obstacles along the way. These six areas can keep you from reaching the financial success you want in your life. Learning how to overcome these six obstacles empowers you to achieve your financial goals and optimize your financial health.

To develop a financial strategy, you must identify where you are in the process and what is keeping you from moving toward achieving your financial goals. You must know where you are starting from, which obstacles are keeping you from financial success, and learn how to overcome them.

The information in this chapter will help you recognize the symptoms and develop the proper strategy to overcome these obstacles. The ultimate prize to financial success is optimizing your financial health and enjoying the financial freedom to live the life you desire.

Figure 1

Diagnosing your financial health empowers you to identify how each of these obstacles impacts your finances. This diagnosis is a key factor in developing the appropriate strategy to win the money game and optimize your financial health. Once the strategy is developed, you must decide, commit, and take action to implement and monitor the strategy to bring your finances to optimal financial health.

The *first obstacle* is the most important one— **mindset/lack of knowledge**. Your perception is reality. Do you have a healthy mindset about money? To be healthy financially, you must have a healthy financial mindset. Does your mindset need to be transformed? No matter what you are trying to accomplish, whether it be to improve your finances or other areas of your life, having the proper mindset is half the battle.

> *Be ye transformed by the renewing of your mind.*
> *– Romans 12:2 –*
>
> *If you change the way you look at things, the things you look at change.*
> *– Wayne Dyer –*
>
> *Finish school, but you should never finish your education.*
> *– Jim Rohn –*

I frequently hear the saying, "You do not know what you do not know." This may be true in other areas, but when it comes to your finances, you usually do know what you do not know. You may be overcome with debt, struggling to pay your bills, or spending more than you make. Whatever the case may be, you know that you need to do something about it.

You may not know the specific strategies to resolve these issues, but you do know that you do not know how to do it. Discover what it takes to resolve your financial problems. Seek guidance and knowledge about what to do to improve your financial situation.

> *My people are destroyed for lack of knowledge.*
> *– Hosea 4:6 –*
>
> *Knowledge is the new rich, arm yourself with it.*
> *– Toni Payne –*
>
> *Knowledge without practice is useless. Practice without knowledge is dangerous.*
> *– Confucius –*

The *second obstacle* is **control over your finances**. Most people do not have control over their finances. Instead of planning where their money goes, they wonder where their money went. Develop a financial plan based on your income, expenses, and spending. Remember, random spending can kill a financial plan. Be a good steward over your finances by planning where your money goes, implementing the plan, and then monitoring and modifying the plan where necessary.

Pay God, yourself, and your emergency fund, in that order. Prioritize your other expenses. Use creative ways to increase your income. Create a plan to reduce expenses and eliminate debt. Establish multiple streams of income. Instead of working for money, make money work for you. You must have a strategy to accomplish these goals.

Well done, thou good and faithful servant: thou hast been faithful over a few things, I will make thee ruler over many things.
— Matthew 25:21 —

It's not how much money you make but how much money you keep, how hard it works for you, and how many generations you keep it for.
— Robert Kiyosaki —

Money is a big part of your life, and when you learn how to get your finances under control, all areas of your life will soar.
— T Harv Eker —

The *third obstacle* is **proper protection**. Many people neglect this area. It is so important to protect your health, life, and finances. A new study from academic researchers found that 66.5% of bankruptcies are the result of medical bills. Surprisingly, 80% of those filers had health insurance.

There is a cost to have health insurance and a cost to use health insurance. They are not the same. You must know the difference. Many people struggle to pay medical bills because of high maximum out-of-pocket amounts, deductibles, copays, minimum coverage, or no coverage at all.

A low premium does not mean you have adequate coverage. One illness or injury can ruin you financially if you do not have the proper protection. Discuss your needs with the Financial Healer to make sure you have adequate coverage for you and your family.

The greatest wealth is health.
– Virgil –

Health is like money. You never have a true idea of its value until you lose it.
– Unknown –

We all know that death is unavoidable, but we still do not prepare for it. We insure our cell phones, homes, and cars but neglect to insure our health and lives. What is more important, these material items or our health and life?

Do not be a liability to your family by leaving them with mounds of medical bills in addition to funeral expenses in the event of your death. Instead, be an asset to your family by acquiring the proper protection that is so much more than money. It provides peace of mind, reduces financial risks, increases financial stability, and secures a financial future for your family.

GoFundMe is not a substitute for life or health insurance. You can get an indexed universal life (IUL) policy that provides three benefits in one product. You get living benefits in the event of a critical or chronic illness or injury; tax-free income for retirement, college, home purchase; as well as the traditional death benefits for the same price as a traditional whole life policy. Speak with the Financial Healer to develop a strategic plan based on your situation to protect you and your family.

> *Risk is like fire: If controlled it will help you; If uncontrolled it will destroy you.*
> *– Theodore Roosevelt –*

> *A good man leaveth an inheritance to his children's children.*
> *– Proverbs 13:22 –*

The *fourth obstacle* is **tax codes and tax laws**. Tax codes such as 401K, IRA, and 403b are part of most Americans' lives. They use these codes to accumulate money to plan for retirement, college education for their children, and the purchase of a home.

These types of investment vehicles are called "qualified plans." This means the investment or seed money is made using pre-taxed dollars. Most people do not realize that when the investment or harvest is withdrawn, it is taxable. Additionally, if they take the money out before the age of 59½, a 10% penalty is imposed on the amount withdrawn. Would you rather pay taxes on the seed or the harvest?

The recent changes in tax laws have significantly impacted middle-class Americans. Deductions that were previously enjoyed have disappeared, resulting in a higher tax liability for this group of people. It is important to have a tax strategy each year to reduce your tax liability.

You should be prepared to ask your tax preparer questions and provide them with all the information that could impact your tax return. If your tax preparer does not ask probing questions before they prepare your tax return, get up and leave. They are likely going to just enter the information and see what results. You can do that yourself.

You want to work with someone who understands the changes in the tax laws, reviews your tax documents, asks probing questions, figures out a strategy, and finds the best-case scenario that results in either an increased refund or reduced tax liability. They should also provide you with a strategy to improve your tax situation for the upcoming tax year.

Do not look for the cheapest tax preparation service. Look for the best. What you save in preparation fees cost you hundreds, or even thousands, of dollars in your refund amount or tax liability for years to come. You usually get what you pay for.

Nothing is certain except death and taxes.
– Benjamin Franklin –

The hardest thing to understand in the world is the income tax.
– Albert Einstein –

The *fifth obstacle* is **investment losses, market risks, and global economic impact**. Most people rely on their financial planner or investment banker to look out for their best interest and monitor the results of their investments and contributions. Most clients make their investments not realizing that the stock market changes multiple times each day.

Invested funds are constantly at risk based on changes in the market. There is a way to get the gains of the market without any risk to your principal or any earned interest—invest your money in products that are indexed to the market. This strategy is discussed later in the book.

We are operating in a global economy. What happens in one part of the world impacts the entire world. As of this writing in summer 2020, we are in a global pandemic that shut down countries around the world. The shutdown impacted the supply chain of every industry, which resulted in less supply to meet demands and higher prices for products and services.

> *A chain is only as strong as its weakest link.*
> *– Thomas Reid –*
>
> *Supply Chain is like nature; it is all around us.*
> *– EverythingSupplyChain.com –*
>
> *More than ever before in human history, we share a common destiny. We can master it only if we face it together.*
> *– Kofi Annan –*

The *sixth and final obstacle* is to **take action**. This obstacle is just as important as the first one. You must decide on a course of action. Commit to a plan. Once you decide and commit to a plan, you must take action to implement the plan. Monitor the results at regular intervals and make the necessary adjustments at the appropriate time. Procrastination and lack of action is a form of insanity.

The acronym A.C.T. stands for Action Changes Things. Take action to empower yourself to change your financial situation for the better. Improve and optimize your financial health.

If you study long, you study wrong.
— Ruby White —

Faith without works is dead.
— James 2:20 —

The distance between what you want and what you get is what you do.
— Mohammed Aathif —

What are your greatest obstacles? Write them down in the order of priority.

1._____
_____
_____

2._____
_____
_____

3._____
_____
_____

4._____
_____
_____

5._____
_____
_____

6._____
_____
_____

Notes

Chapter Two
BASIC TERMS, DEFINITIONS, AND PRINCIPLES

Never underestimate the power of the basics. To diagnose your financial health, there are some basic terms, definitions, and principles you must become familiar with. This book contains terminology that is academic, industry-based, and just plain-old everyday language. Become familiar with all three forms of terminology so you can recognize the impact on your finances. These basics provide a foundation and allow you to strengthen your financial health. In other words, become financially free to live the life you desire.

The main principle is to spend less and keep more of what you make. The objective is to have more income and assets, fewer expenses, and no debt. Let us explore the terms used in the principles of finance. You will see these terms throughout this book as we explore various methods to diagnose your financial health.

Each element will be defined. The examples show how each element impacts another. The objective of this book is to provide essential information to prescribe a financial strategy to optimize your financial health—for you to be in a position where you will not have to worry about money.

Gross Income is the amount of financial gain, earned or unearned, before any deductions are taken. This is the amount you make before taxes and other deductions are subtracted. An example most people are familiar with is the gross income you see on a pay stub.

The calculation of the gross income for a person who works 40 hours/week at a rate of $15/hour is as follows: 40 x $15 = $600 for the week.

Net Income is the gross income amount minus all deductions. This is the amount you actually receive. Let us look at the previous example of a $600 gross income.

The calculation for the net income amount of a person who has deductions from that pay stub includes $120 in taxes and health insurance cost of $80. When you deduct $200 ($120 taxes + $80 insurance) from the gross income, you get a net income of $400. Greater gross income and fewer deductions equal a higher net income.

Pay Cycle is the period in which a recurring payment is due to be paid or received. (e.g., daily, weekly, biweekly, semimonthly, monthly, etc.). In the previous example, the income is calculated for a weekly pay cycle. An example of a billing cycle for payment of a mortgage, utility, phone, etc. is usually monthly.

Expenses are amounts owed for goods or services. There are four types of expenses:

- *Fixed* – the same amount due each cycle (rent/mortgage)
- *Variable* – the amount due changes each cycle (utilities)
- *Unexpected* – not planned but has to be paid (repairs)
- *Temporary* – when the amount due ends after a set period (auto/personal loans). This is also considered debt.

The goal is to minimize expenses as much as possible. We will discuss creative ways to accomplish this in later chapters.

Accrue is when something grows by addition. In the financial world, interest, penalties, and fees accrue. An example of this is a savings account. Accrued interest means you are adding interest to that account balance. When talking about a credit card, accrued interest is being added to the balance owed on the credit card, resulting in a higher balance due.

Debt is when you owe more than you make. Some people overextend themselves by having more financial obligations than they can pay. That is called being in debt. Debt is also a temporary expense when the amount owed can be paid off in full and the expense is no longer required. Once the total amount owed is paid in full, payment will no longer be due.

An example of a debt (temporary expense) is an auto loan. Suppose you purchased a $10,000 car and financed it for 36 months. Your monthly payment is $277/month, which is a monthly temporary expense. Once you pay the last payment of $277 at the end of the 36-month term, the car payments have been satisfied and you no longer have to pay on that debt. The temporary expense/debt is eliminated. That is the ultimate result you are trying to achieve.

I would be remiss if I did not make the distinction between *good debt* and *bad debt*. This is important because understanding this distinction will empower you to make informed financial decisions about whether you take on additional debt.

Good Debt is when you use debt to acquire something that will have equity/value and become an asset once the debt is paid in full. An example of good debt is a mortgage loan on a house or other real estate. Once the mortgage loan is paid in full, the real estate will become an asset with equity.

Bad Debt is when you use debt to purchase things you cannot account for after the purchase is made. You accrue interest on that debt, which increases the amount owed and cannot be recovered. An example of bad debt is when you purchase things like food, clothing, and activities with a credit card and carry the balance beyond the due date. When you accrue interest on those purchases, you are paying more than the original price of the item/activity, which makes those purchases bad debt.

Currency is the method you use to pay for something you purchase. Some people consider cash, checks, credit cards, and lines of credit as the only form of currency. In today's digital world, other forms of currency are becoming more popular and convenient, such as debit cards, payment apps (Apple Pay, CashApp, PayPal, Zelle, etc.), digital wallets, and bitcoins.

When you pay for something with a credit card, pay the balance in full before the next cycle and don't incur interest charges. In this way, it's not considered debt but a currency vehicle that can benefit you in other ways, such as rewards points and cash-back programs, which we'll discuss in a future chapter.

Need is something you *must* have for basic survival. Things like food, a roof over your head, and healthcare are essential for survival. Many people do not consider healthcare a need and do not include the cost in their financial plan. As a breast cancer conqueror, I can assure you that healthcare is a need.

You do not have to have anything as drastic as cancer to feel the pain that one illness, injury, or visit to the hospital can cause to your finances. You must be realistic when classifying something as a need. Ask yourself, "Is this something I must have for basic survival?" If the answer is no, then it is a want and must be classified as such.

Want is something you *desire* but can do without and is not required for your basic survival. Going to the beauty and nail salons, gourmet food, paper towels, and designer clothes are examples of things not essential for your survival.

I did a budgeting workshop at my church and asked the participants to tell me things that were "needs." I got answers like food, electricity, a place to live, medication, etc. One lady shouted out "paper towels." I like to use paper towels, but I explained that you can do without paper towels and still survive. So paper towels are classified as a want. Again, ask yourself, "Is this something I must have for basic survival?" If the answer is no, then it is a want and must be classified as such.

Budget is a summary of expenses allocated for a specific amount of income over a certain period. The word "budget" can be taboo to some people. I like to use the term "strategic financial plan" when referring to a budget because people are more receptive to the thought of strategically planning instead of budgeting. Regardless of how you feel about the terminology, you must plan where your money goes, or else you will constantly wonder where it went after the fact. Creating, implementing, and monitoring your budget is essential to taking control over your finances.

Emergency Fund/Cash Reserves is money saved for future, unexpected, or special uses. One of the most important things you can do is establish an emergency fund when it comes to optimizing your financial health. Having an emergency fund will help you avoid sliding into debt in the event you or your spouse lose your job, need medical care, or must face an unexpected crisis. Setting up an emergency fund is not hard to do but requires some discipline. Figure out what your monthly expenses are and set a goal to save six to eight months of funds in an account you can easily access if needed. Plan to save a full 12 months of funds if you are self-employed.

Spending Habits are determined by how money is spent randomly. These habits are one of the financial vital signs that reveal areas where money is spent unnecessarily. Your spending habits can kill a budget if they are not under control.

One of my clients took the spending challenge and discovered that he was spending over $800/month eating out. This was a wake-up call for him. It was not that he could not afford it, but this made him realize that $800/month can be redirected and used more efficiently in another area of his financial plan. We will delve deeper into this area when we discuss the Spending Challenge.

More money can't fix bad spending habits.
– Beyond a Budget –

Commingle, in terms of finances, refers to mixing personal money with business money. You should have separate bank accounts for your business and personal transactions. They should not be mixed or mingled. If you make a purchase for your business, the proceeds from the business account should be used. Personal transactions should be made from the personal account. This makes recordkeeping clear and concise. Do not mix personal and business money or expenses.

> *A business is not your personal piggy bank.*
> *– Eric Nisall –*

Simple Interest is calculated on the principal alone. An example of this kind of interest is if you have a 2% simple interest rate on $1,000. You would earn $2 every cycle that the interest is paid on the $1,000 principle, resulting in $2 + $2 + $2, and so on.

Compound Interest is interest calculated on the principal plus the accrued interest. Using the same example of a 2% compound interest rate on $1,000, you would earn $2 the first cycle the interest is paid on the $1,000, then you would add that $2 + $1,000= $1,002. The next cycle you would get 2% of $1,002 = $2.00. That would result in $1,002 + $2.00 = $1,004. The cycle continues calculating the 2% and adding it to the principal and accrued interest, and so on and so on.

> *Compound interest is the eighth wonder of the world. He who understands it, earns it... He who does not... pays it.*
> *— Albert Einstein —*

Rule of 72 is the formula that determines the amount of time it takes for your investment to double based on the rate of return (ROR). Figure 2 shows how quickly $10,000 doubles based on the various interest rates.

If you invest $10,000 at a ROR of 4%, you divide 72 by 4. The result is 18. So it will take 18 years for your $10,000 investment to double at a ROR of 4%. If you invest that same $10,000 at a ROR of 10%, you divide 72 by 10 and get 7.2. So it would take 7.2 years for your $10,000 investment to double.

Rules of Money: Rule of 72
Create financial freedom by understanding how your money compounds

4%		6%		8%		10%	
Age	Every 18yrs	Age	Every 12yrs	Age	Every 9yrs	Age	Every 7yrs
34	$10,000	34	$10,000	34	$10,000	34	$10,000
52	$20,000	46	$20,000	43	$20,000	41	$20,000
70	$40,000	58	$40,000	52	$40,000	48	$40,000
		70	$80,000	61	$80,000	55	$80,000
				70	$160,000	62	$160,000
						70	$320,000

How can you earn the higher interest rates without putting your money at risk for market loss?

Figure 2

This formula works the same for credit card debt based on compound interest. Instead of the investment doubling, the debt amount doubles. That is why just paying the minimum amount due on your credit card bill does not reduce the balance. Instead, the balance increases.

	Payment Made	~Time to pay off card	~Total amount of interest paid	~Total amount paid
Full Payment	$1500	1 month	$0	$1500
Partial Payment	$135	1 year	$125	$1625
Minimum Payment	$30	11 years	$1413	$2913

Figure 3

Indexed Investments give you returns based on market activity, with no risk of loss to your principal and earned interest. Investments indexed to the market means your investment is based on market performance but has a ceiling and a floor for your protection. The ceiling caps the amount you receive based on market performance, and the floor prevents any losses if the market drops or crashes.

For example, if your ceiling is 10% and the market return is 12%, you will only receive 10%. The floor is usually zero. If the market goes below zero, your investment stops at zero. You do not make any money, but more importantly, you do not lose any money. Zero is your hero.

Figure 4 shows the comparison of investing $1 in the market and $1 indexed to the market. These are based on actual results from 1998–2017. As you can see, the floor protects your investment from crashing with the market. The person who invested in the market received $2.35. The person who invested indexed to the market received $4.25. What if the investment was $100,000? Which result would you prefer, $235,000 or $425,000?

> *Indexing is a successful approach to investing not because it's simple, but because it has performed so much better than the average active manager (the opposite of indexing), and the simplicity is just an added bonus.*
> *– Patrick Geddes –*

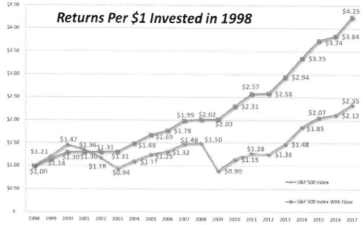

Figure 4

Indexed Universal Life (IUL) is an insurance policy that provides three levels of protection:

- The traditional death benefit that pays your beneficiary when you die.

- Living benefits, which pay you up to 90% of your death benefit in case you live after experiencing a critical/chronic illness or injury.

- The income portion provides you with tax-free income for retirement, college fund, home purchase, or other uses you choose.

The returns are indexed to the market, so you get the growth of the market without the risk of loss to your principal or any earned interest.

Notes

Chapter Three
VITAL SIGNS AND SYMPTOMS

Vital signs are the first source of information the assistant gathers when you go to the doctor. Your temperature, weight, and blood pressure are taken, and the practitioner also asks about any symptoms you are experiencing. This information enables the doctor to properly diagnose your condition and prescribe the proper medication to cure your illness.

The same is true when you see The Financial Healer. To diagnose your financial health, your financial vital signs are taken and noted, which include your income, expenses, and spending. Do you know your financial vital signs? What symptoms are you experiencing? Do you have anorexic income, obese expenses, excessive spending? This information empowers you to know what areas of your finances you need to treat to improve your financial condition.

You cannot heal your finances without knowing the root of your financial problems. Be honest with yourself as you go through this diagnostic process. Working from a realistic view of your income, expenses, and spending is a lot less stressful than planning from a perceived impression of what you think they are.

Looking at your actual financial health, no matter how difficult, might be the motivation you need to improve it. The most important factors are transforming your mindset and behavior as they relate to your finances to optimize your financial health.

Once a financial diagnosis is made, a prescription strategy is recommended to treat your financial illness. The next steps are critical for any effective treatment to work. You must *decide* to improve your financial health; *commit* to the prescribed strategy; and *take action* to implement the strategy to optimize your financial health.

Do you want to have more income, fewer expenses, no debt, and spend less than you make? The ultimate prognosis is to strategically plan where your money goes to take control over your finances; make your money work for you; acquire proper protection to prevent financial ruin; create a financial legacy; create generational wealth; enjoy financial freedom; and live the life you desire. That is optimal financial health.

INCOME

Let us look at your income. Review the income categories in Figure 5 and use it as a guide to identify your income. What sources of income do you have?

List how much money you receive from the various sources, including sources that may not be listed. If you do contract work, odd jobs, or perform other services and are paid cash, keep a written log of the amount and frequency you receive payment. Use the worksheet in Figure 6.

Be realistic. Do not leave any amount out, no matter how small. Be as detailed as possible. Indicate how often you receive the income (daily, weekly, biweekly, monthly, etc.), even if you only received the payment once.

$$$ Income Categories

- Wages/Tips/Contracts
- Business / Hobbies
- Social Security
- Retirement/Pension
- Disability
- Child Support
- Alimony
- Public Assistance
- Unemployment
- Stimulus Payment
- Tax Refunds
- Food Stamps/EBT
- Rental Income
- Interest / Dividends
- Lawsuit Settlement
- Loan Proceeds
- Lottery Winnings
- Casino Winnings
- Gifts/Gift Cards
- Point Rewards/Rebates

Figure 5

Never depend on single income. Make investments to create a second source.
– Warren Buffet –

For example, if you get paid biweekly from your job, receive weekly unemployment benefits, or get monthly social security payments, list each source in the following figure.

Income Sources

Date	Amount	Source	Frequency	Notes	C/CK/DD/ACR*

*C- Cash   CK- Check   DD- Direct Deposit   ACR- Account Credit

Figure 6

Always build multiple sources of income. Never rely on one.
– Universal Royalty –

EXPENSES

Let us look at your expenses. Remember, expenses differ from debt because debt can be eliminated and expenses recur. Use the expense categories in Figure 7 as a guide to identify your expenses—no matter how small. Include expenses not listed in the categories.

Do you pay yourself, contribute to your savings, or pay tithes first? If not, you should.

A good way to identify your expenses is to go through your bank and credit card statements, cash receipts, and any other forms of payment you use.

The *mortgage and loans* categories are debts that can be eliminated once the balances are paid in full. Refer to the categories listed in Figure 7 as a guide to help you identify your expenses. Remember to list every expense even if it is not shown in the category list.

Beware of little expenses. A small leak will sink a great ship.
– Benjamin Franklin –

 Expense Categories

- **Tithes / Savings**
- **Rent/Mortgage**
- **Loans** – auto, personal, bank, credit cards
- **Taxes** – property, auto, personal/income, HOA
- **Insurance** – medical, dental, disability, home, auto, life
- **Utilities** – electricity, gas, phone, cable, internet, security monitoring
- **Childcare** – afterschool, etc.
- **Food** – groceries, lunch (school, work)
- **Transportation** – gas, tolls, bus/train fares, carpool, taxi, parking
- **Copays** – prescription, medical, dental
- **Maintenance** – auto, home, personal (hair, clothes, etc.)
- **Education** – tuition, books, uniforms, computer, supplies
- **Dues** – union, professional, PTA, social
- **Personal Allowance** – cash on hand
- **Travel** – hotel, airfare, meals
- **Recreation** – golf, basketball, football, etc.
- **Habits/Entertainment** – lottery, gambling, smoking, shopping, coffee, dining out, music, apps, subscriptions, games/sports, concerts, movies, etc.

Figure 7

Expenses/Debt

Date	Paid to	Amount	Expense	Debt/Payoff amount	Notes	C/CK/ DD/ACR*

*C- Cash   CK- Check   DD- Direct Deposit   ACR- Account Credit

Figure 8

SPENDING

Spending habits can make or break your financial strategy if not controlled. Things you think you cannot afford can be paid for by redirecting the money you spend on things you want but do not have to have. Do you know how much you spend on non-essential products and services?

Do you eat out for two to three meals a day, buy a $5 cup of coffee per day, buy designer clothes, have a gym membership or subscription you do not use, pay for premium cable channels you do not watch, or purchase other things you want but do not need? You can save hundreds, even thousands, of dollars by controlling your spending.

I challenge my clients to track their daily spending for a month. One client reported that he was spending

$800 per month eating out. These were not for business meals with clients but for personal meals with his wife and grandchildren. It was a real "ah-ha" moment for him. It was not that he could not afford it, but he realized those funds could be redirected to other areas to help him reach his financial goals sooner.

SPENDING CHALLENGE

Take the spending challenge to see how much money you can redirect and use more effectively to reach your financial goals sooner.

> *Discipline is choosing between what you want now and what you want most.*
> *— Abraham Lincoln —*

Track your daily spending by keeping your receipt for every single thing you purchase, no matter how inexpensive. Get a journal and/or envelope to put your receipts in. If you do not get a receipt, log the date, amount, what you purchased, how you paid for it (cash, credit/debit card, check, etc.), and indicate whether it was something you needed or something you wanted.

At the end of each day or week, tally the total amount spent on needs and wants. Multiply the amount spent on wants by the cycle you tallied by (daily, weekly, monthly, annually).

For example, if you spent $5/day on coffee, $15/day on lunch, $4/day on snacks, that totals $24/day times 5 days = $120/week X 4 = $480/month X 12 = $5,760/year on things you can do without.

You can buy coffee and snacks as part of your groceries. Prepare the coffee, lunch, and snacks to take to work or school for less than a quarter of what you spend on these items per year. That is a savings of approximately $4,320/year.

That money can be redirected and used more effectively to pay for essential expenses like health/life insurance, build your emergency fund, pay off credit card debt, or even pay for the family vacation you've been dreaming about.

Don't save what is left after spending, but spend what is left after saving.
– Warren Buffett –

Notes

Chapter Four
CREATIVE WAYS TO INCREASE YOUR INCOME

Most people consider their paycheck, retirement income, and social security benefits as the only types of income. These are known as traditional sources of income. You must think outside the box to increase your income without getting a second job. There are several ways to do this, but you must change your mindset and habits to reap the benefits.

You must set financial goals for yourself. Do not try to set an exact figure. Instead, come up with a general number to serve as a gauge to keep you on track to reaching your goals. Be reasonable and realistic about your target goals. Having an outrageous number will only set you up for failure.

As you see the progress you are making, increase your goals. Likewise, if you are not making progress, revisit your goals and make adjustments. Remember, these numbers are not set in stone. Let us discuss a few ways to use out-the-box thinking to increase your income.

Most people would like to increase their income. Are you leaving money on the table from sources such as rewards, cash-back, and loyalty programs? You can get hundreds, even thousands, of dollars by participating in these programs.

Places where you shop, products that you purchase, and credit/debit cards you use can provide an additional source of income if you take advantage of these programs. Fatten up that anorexic income by making your purchases and money work for you.

CASH-BACK, REWARDS, & LOYALTY PROGRAMS

Take advantage of cash-back, rewards, and loyalty programs for the products, services, and places you frequent. Evaluate your credit and debit cards to see if they offer these kinds of incentives. You can earn cash-back or points that can be redeemed for cash, gift cards, or free services just by doing your routine activities.

I pay my monthly expenses using a cash-back credit card. I earn enough cash back to get hundreds of dollars deposited into my bank account each month. The key to this strategy is to pay off the entire credit card balance each month to avoid paying interest. If you have a debit card that offers cash back, use it for all your expenses and other purchases to receive the cash-back benefits. The money comes directly out of your checking account, so there is no interest.

Make sure you are enrolled in loyalty programs with all the retail, grocery, and online stores, restaurants, airlines, hotels, gas stations, etc. Once you enroll, you can usually enter your phone number or email address to access your account. Check your rewards balance before your next purchase to see if you have enough cash-back, rewards, or loyalty points to redeem toward your purchase. You can save hundreds of dollars that can be redirected for other uses.

COUPONS, FREE TRIALS, DISCOUNTS, AND BOGO

Use coupons, free trial offers, discounts, and buy one, get one (BOGO) promotions. Many stores offer BOGO on certain products, sometimes on a weekly basis. These sources can provide significant discounts on products and services you purchase, which, in turn, increases your income. Many stores reward customers with coupons for free products they purchase frequently.

I receive coupons every month from the grocery store where I shop. Last month, I received coupons for a free 24-pack of water, a box of brand-name cereal, bread, and almond milk. These coupons saved me almost $30 on the items I buy frequently. In addition to these savings, I also earn points toward discounts on gasoline purchases up to $1 off per gallon.

Many services offer free trial periods, usually for 30 days, with no commitment to continue the service after the trial period ends. Services such as Amazon

Prime, Audible, and other membership services provide these offers. The key is to make sure you cancel the subscription before the trial period ends if you choose not to continue the subscription.

A word of caution, most of these types of offers rely on you to subscribe and forget about canceling the subscription. You will then be billed monthly without realizing that you are still paying for a service you are no longer using.

If you are a senior citizen, most companies have discounts and rates designated for seniors. Take advantage of them.

SELL PRODUCTS ONLINE

Most of us have gently used or new products in our home that we have not used or do not need. You can generate cash by listing these items on online sales sites like Offer Up, eBay, Amazon, Etsy, Zulily, and others. My sons generate hundreds of dollars by reselling new and gently used items. We sold my son's car online and got $1,000 more than we expected. We were able to use the proceeds to pay cash for a newer car.

You are surrounded by simple obvious solutions that can dramatically increase your income, power, and success. The problem is you just don't see them.
— Jay Abraham —

As the economy is shifting, you need to have legitimate and creative sources of extra income. There are opportunities available that people have been using for years now.
— Franklin Gillette —

Notes

Chapter Five
REDUCE EXPENSES WITHOUT SPENDING MORE MONEY

Most people suffer from obese expenses. Reducing expenses is usually one of the main prescriptions to treat an obese expense condition—which can be accomplished without spending extra money. You must make expense reduction a goal. As with any goal, you must decide, commit, and take action to reduce your expenses. Here are a few creative ways to accomplish this goal.

As mentioned previously, you must distinguish between an expense and debt. Debt can be eliminated, but expenses recur even after you pay them off in full. A good example of an expense is your utility bill. You can pay it in full each month, but you will have another one the next month, next month, and so on.

An example of debt is a personal loan with a financial institution. The terms of the loan are set for a specific payment amount to be repaid within a determined period. Once the obligation has been met for the specified amount at the end of the determined period, then the loan is paid in full and the debt is eliminated.

AVOID LATE FEES AND PENALTIES

Pay all your bills on time to avoid late fees and penalties. These fees can add up and start to take on a life of their own. If you are living paycheck to paycheck, one late fee can throw everything off. Avoid them like the plague by paying your bills on time. One example of the impact of late fees and penalties is owing the IRS. A tax liability can triple as a result of late fees and penalties. Credit card payments also have significant late fees and over-the-limit fees that impact your balance and the amount of interest you pay if the balance is not paid in full each month. These late fees and penalties continue to snowball if you do not take control.

> *Don't let the fact that you're getting organized result in late fees on your credit card bills.*
> *– Jean Chatzky –*

OVERDRAFT FEES

Overdraft fees are another area that can cost you hundreds of dollars if you let the problem go unchecked. This situation can cause a ripple effect if your bank does not pay the check or electronic funds transfer (EFT) that triggers an insufficient funds fee. Avoid these fees by making sure you have enough in your account to cover the amount issued for payment.

Another safeguard to avoid overdraft fees is to link your checking account to a savings account or credit card that will cover the insufficient amount. This is called overdraft protection. For example, if you write a check for $1,800 and you only have $1,500 in your checking account, the $300 needed to cover the check will be transferred from your savings account or credit card (via a cash advance) to your checking account. You must have enough money in your savings account or enough available credit on your credit card. Additional fees may apply depending on the terms of your financial institution.

> *In 2017, banks made $34 billion in overdraft fees, meaning they made money from people without enough money.*
> *– Unknown –*

EVALUATE AND RENEGOTIATE

Evaluate and renegotiate contracts and services for better rates. This can be done with utility, cell phone, cable, and other companies you do business with. Review your rates at least every six months. Ask your service provider if there are any special rates you qualify for to lower your monthly payments without sacrificing your service level.

I recently called my cable/internet service provider to increase my internet speed. After discussing my needs with the representative, I was able to get faster internet service, more cable channels, keep both my LAN lines, and save $90/month with my new plan.

Additionally, I spoke with my cell phone service provider to upgrade my cell phone. The representative reviewed my account and offered me an upgrade to an iPhone 11 Pro Max and an additional free iPhone 11. I was able to keep my current service level, and I save $150/month with my new renegotiated plan. That is a total savings of $2,880 a year for those two services. What can you do with an additional $2,880?

CANCEL UNUSED MEMBERSHIPS & SUBSCRIPTIONS

Many of us enroll in various memberships and subscriptions and set up recurring monthly payments using a bank account or credit card. We are excited during the initial enrollment period, but as time passes, we stop using the service. The payments continue to get drafted from our bank account or charged to our credit card. We eventually forget about the membership and subscription altogether.

Months go by before we realize that payments are still being made for services we no longer use. More time passes before we take action to cancel the service and stop payments.

Unfortunately, that is what companies count on. They count on us to enroll in the service, stop using it, and continue to pay for something we do not use. This is a critical area where you can reduce your expenses. Cancel these services and redirect those funds from memberships and subscriptions you do not use to pay for expenses you use and need.

The first of the year is when many people enroll in gym memberships to fulfill their New Year's Resolution to lose weight. They show an initial commitment by going to the gym while the excitement is still fresh. By February 1, reality sets in and real-life responsibilities get in the way. Going to the gym gets pushed further down the priority list. Meanwhile, you are paying for a membership you do not use.

You sign up for a 30-day free trial for a service you want to try. The terms say you can cancel at any time. You enter your payment information to get the trial period started and plan to cancel before the 30-day trial is up. You forget all about canceling the subscription and the payment is drafted from your account or charged to your credit card each month.

Cancel those memberships, services, and apps. Redirect that money and use it more effectively to pay for essential expenses. Pay a utility bill, buy groceries, increase your emergency fund, or direct the money to other more essential areas that reduce your expenses.

> *The most important thing is to not waste your money.*
> *— Gareth Bale —*

CONSOLIDATE/ REFINANCE LOANS

If you have a mortgage interest rate of 5% or higher, now is a good time to refinance your mortgage. The interest rates are at an all-time low. You might even be able to pull cash out if you have enough equity to consolidate debt, complete a home improvement project, or use for other debt reduction. The good thing about pulling out some of your home's equity is that the interest on your mortgage is tax deductible (up to the allowable limit).

If you have credit card debt, some credit card companies are offering a 0% interest for as long as 18 months if you transfer the balance from other credit cards. This is a good way to get some interest relief on credit cards with higher interest rates. The money you save can be used to pay off debt or build your emergency fund/cash reserves. You must have good credit to qualify for these programs.

Rewards, Cash Back, Coupons, Discounts, and Offers

Rewards, cash back, coupons, discounts, and offers allow you to reduce the price of your product or service. Join any free program that provides benefits for the products and services you purchase. The following is an example of how beneficial these programs are.

I had to attend a conference in Chicago and shopped for a round-trip, non-stop flight from Atlanta. The cost of the ticket for the times and dates I wanted to fly was about $500 round trip. I was able to use my Southwest Airlines rewards points for the entire flight, and it only cost me $5.60 each way for a total of $11.20 for the entire flight. I was able to check two bags at no charge. That is a huge savings!

Upon arrival, I headed to my hotel. I used my Bonvoy rewards points to book my seven-night stay at the full-service Marriott Hotel in Chicago. I am a loyal Marriott Bonvoy rewards participant and am at the Titanium level, which got me upgraded to a suite. The cost for the stay alone would have cost me in excess of $3,800.

I had access to the exclusive Club Room, where they provided complimentary continental breakfast and evening hors d'oeuvres and beverages. The breakfast menu included smoked salmon, quiche, fresh pastries and fruit, and all kinds of beverages. Ordering those delights in the restaurant downstairs would have cost me at least $50/day just for breakfast. I saved $350 for breakfast alone.

The entire cost of the trip would have been a little over $4,600, but because I took advantage of the rewards points I accumulated with Southwest Airlines and Marriott, my cost was only $11.20.

I do not know about you, but I was able to do other things with that $4,600. Take advantage of these programs and make using them part of your routine. No matter where you go or what you buy, there is a rewards program waiting for you to use.

Money saved is money earned.
– Unknown –

Notes

Chapter Six
CHECK YOUR SIGHT

Check your sight to see how you are looking at your finances. Figure 9 shows the four sights you need to evaluate: hindsight, insight, foresight, and oversight.

Figure 9

Hindsight is always 20/20. Review the choices and decisions you have made, and the actions you have taken. What were the results? Were they positive or negative? What did you learn from them? If you could do things differently, would you? If things went right, that is great—keep doing them. If it did not go right, what lessons did you learn from the experience? Have you identified areas that need changes? Are you willing to make those changes? What impact will those changes make?

Have a "pity party" if you need one, but do not stay there long. Do not beat yourself up about it but learn from it. Change your behavior and mindset and move forward with a better attitude and discipline to achieve your financial goals.

> *In hindsight everything is much clearer.*
> *– Bart Cumming –*

> *Forgive yourself for not having the foresight to know what now seems so obvious in hindsight.*
> *– Judy Belmont –*

Insight is a clearer and often sudden understanding of a complex situation. Step back and see the big picture and the results you want. Interpret and respond to your present situation. Systematically gather information and update your strategy to achieve your financial goals.

> *The secret of change is to focus all of your energy, not on fighting the old, but on building the new.*
> *– Socrates –*

Foresight is planning for the future, seeking possible opportunities, observing warning signs, and preventing threats to a perceived outcome. Plan ahead with the lessons learned from your hindsight and the perspective gained from your insight.

> *Foresight is not about predicting the future; it's about minimizing surprise.*
> *– Karl Schroeder –*

Oversight is about putting processes in place to monitor progress and identify, prioritize, and manage critical risks to assure the success of your financial strategy. Basically, there must be checks and balances in place to prevent a major impact on your finances. When you identify a risk or threat to your finances early enough, you can do something about it and prevent financial ruin.

A good example is having adequate health and life insurance in the event of illness, injury, or death. Another example is having alerts and two-step verifications set up on your bank accounts and other service accounts. Identity theft is becoming a problem in today's technological and cashless-driven society.

The lesson is the importance of never becoming untethered to oversight and accountability.
— James Comey —

In the age of information, ignorance is a choice.
— Unknown —

There is only one limitation to our progress and that is our lack of information.
— Sunday Adelaja —

Notes

Chapter Seven
WHAT IS YOUR DIAGNOSIS?

Now that you have completed the exercises in this book, what have you discovered about your financial condition? Are you satisfied with your financial health? Do you understand why your finances are in the shape they are in?

Do you have anorexic income? Obese expenses? A spending addiction? Insufficient knowledge? Poor mindset? Lack of proper protection? Overweight tax liability? Hemorrhaging retirement and investment vehicles? Have you contracted the global financial pandemic? Are you crippled by inaction?

If you are suffering from any of these conditions, make an appointment with The Financial Healer to discuss your condition. The Financial Cures System™ has the right prescription and therapy to cure your financial ills.

Sometimes it's not about the money, but rather the process of managing the money.
  – Freshly Married –

List the areas of concern you want to address.

_____
_____
_____
_____
_____
_____
_____

You must gain control of your money OR the lack of it will forever control you.
— Dave Ramsey —

Ascend from where you are to where you want to be.
— Dr. Wendy Labat —

Notes

CONCLUSION

Most people want financial security but do not know how to achieve it. I pray that the information in this book has provided you with some guidance and information that will empower you to get a true diagnosis of your financial health. Do not get discouraged by what you see. The journey will not be easy, but the reward will be worth it.

You need a team of professionals to achieve optimal financial health. Do your homework to find the right people and know the right questions to ask. Get referrals from people you know and trust. Make sure the people you are considering to become a part of your team have firsthand knowledge and experience in their field of expertise. This team should begin with a financial strategist, insurance agent, tax professional, lawyer, and banker. As your financial situation improves, you can add to your team based on current and future needs.

Most wealthy people did not start that way. They had to develop the right mindset and discipline, work hard, and make sacrifices to take control over their finances. They acquired the proper protection to prevent financial ruin and used it to create generational wealth.

Wealthy people have multiple streams of income and avoid market risks and investment losses. They make money work for them. Most importantly, they decide, commit, and take action.

If you don't find a way to make money while you sleep, you will work until you die.
— Warren Buffett —

Sometimes you have to take two steps back to take ten forward.
— Nipsey Hussle —

Don't be afraid of growing slowly, be afraid of standing still.
— Dr. George C. Fraser —

Notes

94 Diagnose Your Financial Health

ABOUT THE AUTHOR

Dr. Wendy Labat, aka The Financial Healer, is an award-winning entrepreneur, strategist, speaker, and best-selling author. She has her Doctor of Business Administration (DBA) degree in Entrepreneurship and over 36 years of experience as an entrepreneur. Dr. Labat is the CEO of The Financial Cures LLC, a financial strategy and business development firm. She also serves as the Founder and CEO of Ascend Foundation Inc., a 501(c)3 nonprofit organization, established to empower disadvantaged women to realize their dreams of entrepreneurship.

Dr. Labat shares the knowledge, experience, and wisdom garnered firsthand from the challenges she faced starting a business 36 years ago, with no business experience, limited financial resources, and most recently, conquering breast cancer. This journey led her to develop The Financial Cures System™ (TFCS), which she has used to improve the financial lives of many entrepreneurs, business owners, families, and individuals across the U.S.

She empowers her clients to formulate specific strategies to diagnose their financial health; take control over their finances; make their money work for them; acquire proper protection to prevent financial ruin; build a financial legacy; create generational wealth; and become financially free to live the life they desire. Dr. Labat wrote *Diagnose Your Financial Health* to get people started on their journey to optimize their financial health.

Dedicated to her community, Dr. Labat also serves on the Board of Directors of the Zion Hill Community Development Corporation, providing housing for homeless senior women and young adults, and is an active member of Zion Hill Baptist Church. Dr. Labat serves on the Community Action & Business Ministry charged to assist with Voter Registration, Healthcare Enrollment, Financial Literacy, and the 2020 Census count. During her career, she has served as a Board Member for various business and civic organizations.

In addition to being one of the authors of *The Lemonade Stand: Book 2*, Dr. Wendy Labat has been featured in publications such as *Success Profiles Magazine, Authority Magazine, Lemonade Legend Magazine, Black Enterprise,* and *The Atlanta Tribune,* to name a few. She is featured in the 50th Anniversary PBS American Portrait broadcast. Additionally, Dr. Labat was inducted into the Marquis Who's Who as Top Entrepreneur/Business Owner.

FREE GIFT

To schedule a complimentary 20-minute strategy session with The Financial Healer, text "Talk" to 770-796-4944.

Notes

Made in the USA
Columbia, SC
22 October 2020